Melba Peña

Lost Between Wanting & Able

Order this book online at www.trafford.com
or email orders@trafford.com

Most Trafford titles are also available at major online book retailers.

Printed in the United States of America.

ISBN: 978-1-4669-2600-4 (sc)
ISBN: 978-1-4669-3363-7 (e)

Trafford rev. 05/29/2012

www.trafford.com

North America & international
toll-free: 1 888 232 4444 (USA & Canada)
phone: 250 383 6864 ♦ fax: 812 355 4082

Contents

Chapter 1

Introduction

Well the truth of the matter is, I fell in love with poetry in my Junior year. In my Senior year we moved to Trona, CA. I didn't mind because I did not fit in at that time. I saw myself as an under achiever born to a family of over-achievers and cousins who were all going to grow up to be teachers and administrators. I was a lazy child and did not always put my best foot forward.

I liked Trona from the first moment I saw it. It was like visiting a SyFi movie. The ground resembled craters, like on the moon. At first sight it gave you a wrong impression of where you were. My outer appearance was also not revealing as to who I was. It may sound strange, but I felt we were both misunderstood and both had mysteries to hide. We were not how others saw us. We fit just like a hand in a glove.

When I was told which classes I was going to have to take, I became filled with angst when told Creative Writing. I had hopes of trying to be a writer but strong anxieties about not having the flair or style to be the exceptional writer I wanted to be. My grammar was very poor and my spelling was terrible. However, I loved reading Earnest Hemingway, William Faulkner, Edgar Allen Poe, Emily Dickenson and William Ernest Henley.

However, I did not continue to write. Life for me began early. I married two years after graduating and had three children. At 50 years I was diagnosed with Parkinsons. However this was my chance to try writing again. But there is no fairytale ending. I did not hit it big or make money writing. I just love to write and have a great deal to say. Whether I make a name for myself or not, I will write because I love writing. My reward is hearing if my writing reached a reader enough to bring a strong emotion. To bring a response, reaction or perhaps a good laugh would be sufficient.

My first book "Life's Rhapsodies" is very special to me and is full of strong emotions of love lost. It reflects on memories of family and friends. It also includes a few children's poems. It expresses my heritage and my love for this country. There is also a little humor.

Alouicious—Protector of the Weak was written for my daughter as a children's book based on a poem that is in my first book as "The Teddy Bear Massacre of 1996". Alouicous was a Teddy bear that my daughter was very close to while she was ill and confined to a hospital bed for several months. She grew up with him and wanted him immortalized as a live playmate that was there for her when in need. They are still together as close friends.

To The Wise One

Daddy, Daddy why are you so cranky?
You're only 90 yrs old with a heart that is full of Gold.
You fought June 6, 1944 in Normandy Omaha Beach and
was part of the 3rd wave of the invasion.
Imagine the gift you were given that day to make it through
such a horrendous day.

The multitude that died that day, God chose you to stay
What a blessing he gave to you and to two little girls
that were waiting to be born and celebrate the gift you were
given.
Fulfillment, celebration, love and treasures sealed your duffle
bag;
even though the bag was stolen your treasure has survived
these 90 yrs.

Your health, your mind, your joyful laughter
Brings satisfaction to all you meet.
You're instantly loved by the ones you touch
and happiness is surrounding you and those
who are close enough to view your smile.

So Daddy, Daddy
where's that smile
that God so
graciously gave you?
Please share it with
me today
so that I can pass it
to others who
wait to share it too.

From the Wise One

A little history to the grandchildren about Great Grandpa. He received the Campaign medal with 5 Bronze Stars, a Good Conduct medal, World War II Sharp Shooter Medal, Presidential Unit Citation and the French Fourequire.

Papa Marco landed at Omaha Beach in Normandy on July 9, 1944. As part of the 3rd wave on the beaches. They went first to a small town St. Mere Eglise that had been liberated by the 82 Airborne Division. The objective of the 2nd Armored Division was to secure the town and move on to Saint Lo. The German 7th Panzer Army occupied the city and it also needed to be secured. From there they traveled to the Seine River and then we liberated Paris. From there we took the Netherlands and were attacking the Sigfried line to cross into Germany. On December 19th we were relieved and sent to Belgium where the Germans had surrounded the 101 Airborne Division at Bastongne. The attack there was on December 23, 1944 under General George Patton. This was a big battle that lasted three weeks. The Germans were defeated, then we went back under General Bradley and crossed the Sigfried line into Acchen and attacked Cologne. A huge battle developed trying to cross the Rhine River. Then finally made it to Dusseldorf and went on to Heidelberg, and Magdeburg by the Elbe River.

The World War II peace treaty with Germany included the Russians and the US Allies was signed in Berlin with a big parade on May 8, 1945. After the signing of the treaty, there was a parade that included President Truman, Winston Churchill, General De Gaulle and the Russian Dictator Stalin.

We served as guards on the American side of Berlin that bordered with the Russian Sector. Many incidents occurred with the Russians because many Germans wanted to come to the American side. We stayed in Berlin until November 1945 and was shipped home in December of 1945.

Three years later your Grand Mother was born.

Life

prevails
affliction

suffering and trials
surrounding you with zest
it strengthens through grief and care

"existence conducts energy"

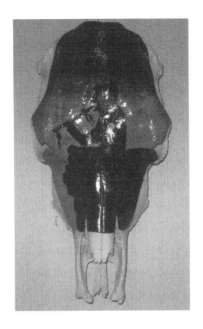

The Essence of Me

The many faces of me
are kept so well hidden
that no one else
can see their presence.

For I embrace
many generations that
come to life within me,
and I through them.

My parents are the strongest part of me
for they are the closest
and have built my foundation
for which I am thankful.

The lineage continues with
my grandparents.
They all live within me
each absorbing a part of me.

I duplicate them all in life and spirit.
In my essence there is a trace of
their existence and when my time is gone,
I will continue to emit my presence.

Like Clint

Body aches,
right side shakes,
carrying a few extra pounds.

Want to do things
like yesterday,
and try till the pain
holds you down.

Your mind is willing;
your body falters.
You're lost between
wanting and able.

When you can, try again
if you can't, then rest.
You've never been a quitter.

Old age is a pain
that can wear you out,
but a body filled with
impairment, will leave you
aching
without due pleasure.
There's nothing to do but
face it,

So be like a TV hero.
There is nothing to say, but
"Do you feel lucky? Well do
ya?" and
"Go ahead, Punk, make my
day."

Aging

Too old for this
too young for that
I was left stuck in the middle.
My light bulbs work,
they still glow bright,
but there is a short in the wire.
My wheels still are spinning
but they're losing their traction.
I'm thrashing in mud,
so look out for the splashing.
You don't want to be the attraction.
My cushion's still good,
there's plenty of padding.
For the breaks that I take,
I need soft and charming.
Come sit down a spell.
There's room for your cushion
which, might I say, is *"flushingly"* nice
for someone who's stuck in the middle.

Before the Curtain is Drawn

I'm slowly forgetting the simple things
like teasing, playing and singing in key.

I don't even laugh like I used to do.
My mouth doesn't curl up to smile anymore.

My once sparkling eyes are losing their glitter.
My nerves are always up in a flutter.

I'm never content. I just want to vent.
I'm not even able to spring plant.

My time clock is running too fast.
My legs can't keep up with the task.

I still want to play and mold something in clay,
or perhaps paint like Picasso.

I don't want to stop the essence of me.
I want to create, not deteriorate.

What should I do to bring in some life
before the curtain is drawn?

Dancers

The shadow dancers have returned with the darkness
to haunt me and taunt me through the night,
but they don't frighten me or sadden me as the dancers
flowing from the shore and following through daylight.

Dancers dance for me at night
show me tumult through daylight,
show me your dazzle in the candlelight
or show me your sadness in the blackest night.

Oceans show me beauty in color blue,
then show me sorrow in twilight hue.

Dark Clouds

Dark clouds slowly come to absorb me
In the form of a dark black veil,
which wraps and tangles tightly round.
I can't free myself for I'm brutally bound.

My legs are completely consumed.
No need to struggle or fight,
I'd like to resist but my muscles are weak,
and I feel that the outcome is bleak.

I dream that perhaps things can change.
The dark clouds could fade and abstain.
If they don't, I am trapped like a fly in a snare,
and I can't free my mind for my body's ensnared.

How long will this torment keep?
Do they all think I'm dead or asleep?
Like the fly in a web, I see someone is there
as my mind cries out, "I'm still here!"

Like a corpse in a coffin I lay,
oblivious to what they may say,
I'm nether alive nor clinically dead,
just cloaked by absorbing dark clouds.

Darkness

The nights keep getting darker,
the rain keeps falling harder,
faces keep getting colder,
and I keep growing older.

My heart is weary from all my struggles,
to redeem myself from all my troubles.
If only my heart could be of stone,
then maybe I could live alone.

Survive a world where I don't belong,
survive a life that does not exist,
believe in truths that never were,
forget your words that wound me still.

Despair

We've become quite old friends.
You visit me often,
as some loyal friend.
You cater to me like some special child.
My company is pleasing to you.

Fools have always been your prey,
so here I am,
ready for you to devour me,
as I struggle no more.

Let your pain consume me.
You have a home within me,
with a lifetime guarantee
of more to come.

Friend your name is *Despair*.

The Blues or the Blahs

When the day starts poorly
and continues on its negative way,
I crawl back in bed
and cover my head.

My curtains are drawn
the room in a glum
just feeling the blues
or maybe the blahs.

What makes me feel
sad and wanting the dark?
Was it something you said
or something you did not?

I know I'm not ill,
The world is in a frazzle
I feel upside down
I shake like a tassel

Was it you? Was it me?
What is this thing in me?
Was I just hoping
for someone to say,
Gee!
How about
"Job well done!"

How I like my bed,
the fluffy large pillow
that cradles my head.

If I keep silent
tomorrow will come
with the bright sunlight beaming.
I'll welcome the dawn.

I Feel The Same Way

What do you see when you look at me?
A helpless, mindless, decrepit being,
a worthless person broken and lost,
inside my shell imprisoned and numb.

Do you see me less able because I shake?
Unable to think or speak for myself,
sadly enough, I feel the same.
I look at the world as it's always been.

I still want to dance, converse and play,
like I did before I became encased,
in this damaged receptacle-occupying space.
I want you to see me like I'm full of grace.

I see you the same as you pass my way,
but you hustle hurriedly, no time to stay.
Have my tremors and slothful walk made you look away?
Or is my slow movement inconvenient for you?
Has the softness of my words become a nuisance too?
Wow, that's funny, I feel the same way.

Dead End

Floating along like deadwood,
in a stormy sea of dreams
targeted only by the deadeye
exposed to the burning heat.

Deadlocked by the choices confronting me
while the deadlines expire
and the deadlight calls me
to finish my time left in dead space
and my dead receptacle.

Rhapsody

I have traveled this road many times before. I remember it when I was young and strong. The road was smooth and flat beneath a light blue sky. It enticed me with adventure and sights so filled with *Rhapsodies*. What a glorious road it was. I was able to run, skip and of course walk this road when it came calling. It filled my soul with awe and wonder, satisfying my hunger to explore.

As my life has journeyed on, I again have come to this same road I have traveled on before. It was a little worn and haggard from the years gone by. There was an occasional crack in the pavement, a puddle of rain here and there, a few weeds making their way through the black top, and the blue sky was occupied by dark gray clouds. I no longer wanted to run and skip or hunger to explore, but cautiously searched the scenes of *Rhapsodies* once more.

This road does change with time, as I journey still again. The road remains worn and haggard from the span of time, yet the flowers still host their blooms in spring. The trees still offer their welcomed shade. The occasional rain brings the moisture back to the earth. Though the cracks in the pavement can lead me to fall, and the occasional puddles will wet my feet, there is still a *Rhapsody* playing and calling to me.

Truths of Life

When I was not so very old, maybe about 13 years . . . a young girl; I got so mad at God, my Lord because He did not hear my prayer.

I was so close to my Grandpa, he was the world to me. I prayed so hard and prayed so long, but God still set him free. My heart was torn. My eyes flooded me whole. I said, "You told me Lord, I only needed to ask." I asked . . . I thought, You heard my words as I cried out to You. I told all my friends at school that I prayed for You to save him, but You let him die. Now all I do is cry. They must have thought how silly I was to believe You could keep him from dying. Or maybe the word is "would" not "could." How is a child to know? Other's said," let him go. He is in such pain. God was being merciful to let him go. Don't be sad for him. He is not suffering now. It's you that is hurting now, so just cry for yourself and be glad for him."

How could they say that to me? I was not being selfish. They did not understand that I loved him, oh so much. You left me feeling hopeless. My faith was badly shattered. Why did You forsake me? You did not hear my prayers.

But it was I that did not hear, His answer to my prayer. So my heart went cold and closed the door to never hear Him answer.

I then grew up keeping my distance from God's promises. It is just a book.

Why should we care? It has no power in it, yet . . . why did my Grandmother continue to walk close to Him? She never left his side. She never questioned

or asked Him why?

We never spoke about my anger, she just knelt and prayed daily. Her faith in God was gigantic. Her love for Him divine. I could not pretend I did not see her faith growing stronger. But she didn't ever force the words that were printed in my Book. I just saw her glowing more each day as the days went by. God was growing inside her and now she had lovingly passed it to me. I received her many blessings

without even knowing when they came. I thank God for her blessings and never giving up on me.

One day, many years later, she saw my book of poetry. Though I still had kept my heart closed, when I wrote these words in a poem about a man searching for the truths of life and mysteries unspoken. Yet . . . finally he died under a tree, alone but holding the Holy Bible.

"Did he find what he was looking for in this Holy Book or did he die floating in the mystery?"

My grandmother held the book and asked? "What book was it he had?

Was it God he was searching for in this black book?"

"Yes, grandma the book was the Holy Bible. He searched his whole life for the truth and why there were unspoken mysteries. Even this, he finally knew. He finally listened to what he had prayed for and why the mysteries were untold."

"He died after decades of searching, but I will die without any questions or tears for I know now where your strength comes from and why your tears brought you relief and not anger, and my heart is open and free for I will see God, you, and those we love in Heaven after our tomorrows."

I realized after all those years my grandmother never questioned my reasoning, but faithfully prayed for my understanding and submission to God's will. I'm glad my Grandmother was faithful, steadfast with tenacity, and I thank God for her unyielding faith. She was the anchor of the family and God's vessel of Love. She spread His word of Love and Hope to those who wished to listen,

but she never gave up on those who didn't want to hear God's word. She never scolded using His word but lived her life as God's will commanded. Just being His example saved more souls than if she would have tortured them. She just lived as God told her and the rest all just followed.

Like A Dove

Spirit of the light
come to me in flight
like a dove in gentle breeze
and free me from the night.

My eyes are sightless now
but seek your radiant glow
send down your beaming dove
and fill me with your love.

Let the darkness flee
like a leaf caught by the wind
transcending all that yields it
to reside and then decay.

Open up my eyes
and guide me to your light
let me soar to you with wings
like the dove in gentle breeze.

Circle's End

Another night
I sit by the window and watch
the sun going down
you're not around.

When will this circle end
everyday it turns out the same
will it end in the dark on a hot August night.

Mornings are bad
I sip my coffee and watch
the sun glide up to the clouds
I still listen for your sound.

When will this circle mend
everyday remains the same
when will it lose its' grip.

The day is full of nothing
no conversation or warm embrace
the sun just glares through my eyes
you're not around.

The circle must be broken
no special gift or surprise to look forward to
it never changes
how will it end.

It'll end with me
when it's time to leave
and I am free.

Loneliness Is

Loneliness is not tested in an empty room
but seen profoundly in a crowded one.

Loneliness is not best seen when all alone
but when surrounded by people you know.

Loneliness is not always destructive
Sometimes it's constructive.

Loneliness is not always debilitating
sometimes it's illuminating.

Why Do I Suffer So?

Sometimes I feel I can't bear the weight of the world on my shoulders. My legs tremble from pressure given from each and every painful moment I have seen. I need not know my brother or my sister to feel their pain, like the weight that is slowly crushing me. God, why do I suffer so? I see such cruelty. I see the torment. I hear the innocent crying "have mercy." I see the unborn waiting in the darkness, hoping to be born into this loveless world. There is no beauty where flowers should bloom, no laughter where little mouths should sound their joyful voice to the world. Where goes the gentle breeze and tender touch, the once spoken audible words? Lord, You are the Master and the Keeper of my soul. Why does the pain of the world fall upon me? Why do I see what others cannot? Why do I feel what others will not? I am just a simple being with no special gifts.

If a small beast of no importance runs in the path of mortal danger, I feel its pain as if it were my own, and tears flow with tremendous sorrow. Tomorrow may be better, but for now the creature has my tears.

In blackness I lay and pretend to sleep, but the world is still weighing me down. My breathing is labored from the crushing pain of the weight that's still resting on me. I see illness and famine, wars and destruction. The devil is sharpening his claws. Oh Father, where are you? The devil is lurking. He wants to take all of our souls. He preys on the negligent that do not watch the changes appearing today. But if You continue to show us the signs, I know he'll not have mine. We'll thrust the beast to where he belongs, beneath the pits of Hell.

I Don't Want To

I don't want to think too hard
I just want to fall apart.

I don't want to make a plan
to get through this odious span.

I just want to cry all day
not even think of why, I say.

This is just too much to face
so would you please just go away?

Patient's Prayer

Woke up this morning, my body in pain.
I thought, "Oh Lord, let me make it through another day,
without seeing the doctor, give me relief.
I dread the speech she'll have ready for me."

I'll tell her my symptoms, she'll almost accept
that everything I'm feeling is all in my head.
But the truth of the matter, it all really is
locked tight in my brain concealed from her sight.

She'll chew on her pencil then look at me stern
like I'm in pre-K on my first day of school.
"Have you been taking your medicines on time?
Did you eat well?" Like she really did care.

She then makes eye contact. "Democrats are at fault
Our healthcare is spiraling on a downward slope."
Lowering her voice, "It's going to get worse.
Better tell our congressman, Medicare and Medicaid
are not fair at all, to the doctors who studied
to prosper from pain.

Throw them out if their ill or their bodies impaired.
No money or insurance, their life span is spent."
Somebody tell her, that time is at hand. I mean,
Medicare and Medicaid are not welcomed we've seen.
No help for the weary or patient's in pain.
Don't schedule these patient's the doctors proclaim.

While the patient's lie dying, the physicians engulfed
by the working, middle class, blue collar mass
that struggle to keep their jobs and medical needs,
our healthcare is not working, it needs some reform.

The Republicans blame the Democrats,
the Democrats say whoa!
We haven't even started, just wait until we fail.
The important thing is the patient might one day be you
or maybe your son or daughter may need treatment too.

We must stop quarreling and find some relief
and ask Lord, heal the physician and Lord heal me too.

Chapter 2

A New Beginning

In times of turmoil and chaos, You lift me up so that I may see the calm, peacefulness and the clear blue sky. There is always tomorrow.

In times of self-absorption and egoism, You bring me below my self-importance and show me the critical state to which some must surrender. They must find solace in their accomplishments though not completed.

In times of self-pity, You remind me that I am given choices in life, and my choice of direction could have brought me blindly to this state of depression.

In times of boisterous laughter, You clear my heart from the weight and pain we tend to hold on to. Release acquires relief.

In times of sadness, we flood the ground with our well-hidden tears of regret and tormenting sorrow, thus renewing all; beginning the cycle again.

All because You lifted Your son from the turmoil, egoism, self-pity, boisterous laughter and sadness that man could create; You gave us all a new beginning.

Deeds and Words

If I could see the error of my deeds
like I see my face in a mirror.
I know that I would choose other ways
to complete my thoughts and my actions.

If I would listen to how my words are said,
I would probably beg for forgiveness.
But since I don't always do what is best,
I shall ask you Lord for mercy.

A Time to Sow

God starts my day off well.
The sun is shining, yet cool right now;
I plant the seeds to feed us.

I know the work is very hard.
I tire, hunger and later feel
the pain of a long hard day.

The soil could use a little moisture.
It's hard under my feet,
still I grumble about this,
when God has set a time to sow.
His time is never wrong.

The day is good.
I can't complain.
I gratefully have seeds to plant.

I praise you Lord.
You are my strength,
with you my seeds will grow.

A Wish

I wish for you true happiness and the knowledge
To recognize it when it happens,
For it won't be as you expect.

I wish for you the ability to give love completely
And honestly without the thought
Of oneself or personal gain.

I wish for you the gift of receiving love
For its' simplest form of one caring for you
Just as you are.

I wish for you love and not wealth
Because love will prevail when wealth is gone
And love holds happiness forever.

As I Commit

When others cry, why me dear Lord,
I know that plea can't be answered.
So I just pray, help me Lord,
you chose the path I'll follow.

When the pain is grave I cannot face it,
I cover my eyes and cry,
to you Lord I give you praise
and ask you to light my way.

Send me love and consolation,
bring me close to your salvation.
Thank you for your precious blessings
as I commit myself with love.

Faith

Each day I awake and I know
that whatever happens this day
I will manage to handle.

I will be fed.
I will have shelter
and if tragedy strikes
I will survive its brutality.

When friends forsake me,
I hold my head high,
because I know who is with me.

If I wish to cry without
knowing why,
that too is alright, because I
will not perish
from despair, for You will
not forsake me.

When others try to cause me
pain,
You spread Your wings to
shelter me.
When battles rise to make
me struggle
You send Your armies to
fight for me.

You keep me out of peril.
You never leave me hanging.
You keep my spirits high.
Even coming to the end
You'll come to take me
home.

My Daydream

When I daydream
I am many things
that I fail to be
In my dreams at night.

I am confident and accomplished.
Where I chose to be is where I set my compass,
without apprehension of how others will see me.

When I daydream
I see myself tranquil and carefree.
No disappointments worry me
for I stand by my beliefs.
No threats of who I shouldn't be.
I am all that I strive,
never swaying from my path,
I am true to myself and
therefore you can trust
I will be true to you.

Maybe Then I'll be A Poet

I'd like to be a writer, known for my witty tales
that excite the mind and bring a tear just once in a while.

Can you feel me? And see me? Can you perceive the pain I
express?
Or are my thoughts just floating, disguised as a breath of air.

A little snip of laughter to liberate your heart
would please me greatly, if I could just grant that gift to you.

A dash of compassion expressed so delicately
may lend a hand to kindness.

While anger is sometimes necessary
to release the child in you.

All humanity is alike, believing in similar truths.
Yet, we go on as strangers, not seeing or regretting what we do.

We close our eyes, cover our ears, and probably should muffle
our words,
for tomorrow we'll see what we have sown, with our senseless
deeds.

If I could free one despondent
person, calm a broken heart,
expand an act of kindness,
and release the child in you.

Maybe then I could say, I am
a poet
a true composer of words.

Moon Glow Solitude

Sitting, thinking, almost dreaming
I saw the moon begin to rise.
Its hue was full of grandeur.
Its perfect roundness and breathtaking size
did suddenly catch my eye.

"What a lover's moon you are.
Your moon glow leaves me wanting
and gasping to share your light
And the warmth you send down tonight."

"What's that you say?
You're wanting and gasping too?
How can that be? You're so like me.
Regretting the solitude."

"Well, let me be the first to say,
no one compares with you.
You've been forever giving of your light
And set the mood for countless nights."

"Don't look so sad, you've never failed.
A fortress strong you've been.
Your beauty blankets the planet complete
None surpassing your mystery and light,
or the way you look tonight."

With Praise I Pass It On

Christmas is almost here
the days have turned cold and icy.
The memories of childhood
Christmas's
flood my mind and make me
smile.

Thank you God for Jesus
and his strength to die for us.
Because of You, I feel so loved
that You could sacrifice Your
Son

How giving you are and so I
should be, filled with the love
You faithfully give
and share it with those
that never may know,
How peaceful and warm
Your love can be.

So from my heart to yours dear
God, I send my love back to you;
With praise and Thanks
for your selfless gift . . .
You've shared with all
mankind.

Now I will try to do what's right
and share your love with all
in need.

Weeds

Weeds sprout without food or water,
they need no nurturing, sunlight or warmth.
Weeds spread and overrun a garden,
multiple and thrive through harshest times.

You cannot kill them totally
for they come back every year,
to strangle and to suffocate
the flowers as they bloom.

So like the weed that sets its roots well planted in the earth,
an evil seed can plant itself way deep inside your thoughts,
taking control of your desire, and taking away your mind,
making you do and say things you hoped you never would.

It spreads its thorns to all around, to hurt, maim and kill.
Be vigil, pray to God, and keep this seed away.
Be kind, be loving, be true, and you will always be
like a garden full of blossoms and no weeds can leave their
seed.

The Seed of Hope

I've chosen my own paths to walk
some hard and unappealing.
They've cost me quite a price to pay
with shame and degradation.

Yet still the sun comes up again
and offers me new light.
to make myself all over again
and plant a seed of hope.

Then when it's time to lay my head
there will be no tears of shame.
For I walked this day with God in hand
And will rise the new day smiling.

Your Shroud

The roads I traveled on
were rugged and rocky
dry, dusty and narrow
As I traveled on
the roads I've traveled on
were dangerous and slippery
were dark and mysterious
Your shroud kept me hidden.
from the demons that lurk
by the road to find lost souls
never knowing the dangers were
there, still, I've always been saved

by Your Grace and Your Glory.
You kept me in spite of myself.
I give You praise, adoration and
gratitude for you saved me from myself.

The Rain

This morning as I awoke, I heard loud thunder crack the sky. The rain came pouring down like blankets of puddles. So in this time of turmoil, I couldn't help but wonder, did God send this rain to cleanse my soul, to start me fresh all over again? Did he make the thunder crack so loud that I would listen? Did my soul need rejuvenation?

I pondered sleepily as I listened to the rain. The alarm now sounding with the thunder telling me it's time to rise. The rain kept its steady rhythm and never missed a beat. Then it came to me why God sent the rain. He sent it to hide my sorrow so that no one could see or question my sadness if a tear should fall. That must be why God sent the rain.

I made the bed and drank my coffee, watching the clouds grow darker. The lightening now joined in song with the rain and thunder, showing its elegance as it danced through the sky. It filled my soul with renewed spirit. I rushed to get dressed and went, out to join God's melodic creation.

No, God didn't send the rain to wash my sins, or to hide my tears. He sent the rain to tickle my toes, to wet my nose and splash my hair with droplets. He made the thunder to make me listen to the music it created and the lightning that danced with such paramount elegance that I might pause in wonder. He made the rain for me to see that all that is can be washed away.

Free, Wistful and Majestic

Songbird
sitting in the tree, what's that song you're singing
so blissful and so free?
Did I ever sing like you, contented and fulfilled?
Songbird, teach me how to sing.

Eagle
Soaring through the clouds, playing with the wind
In a graceful, wistful dance.
Did I ever dance like you, with beauty and elegance?
Eagle, teach me how to dance.

Robin
red breast showing proud, you flaunt your colors gloriously
and strut yourself majestically.
Did I ever feel like you gratified and impervious?
Robin, teach me how to pose.

Yes, I'll sing just like a songbird
romancing every note.
My heart still aching so
I'll sing just like a songbird.

Yes, I'll dance just like the eagle
loving every move.
My soul will see me through.
I'll dance just like the eagle.

Yes, I'll pose just like the robin,
proud of who I am.
And sure I look so grand.
I'll pose just like the robin.

So be happy with who you are
Sing the song within your soul
And bring it from the heart
Then it will surely show.

Dance and move with your own grace
No one can emulate the way you move
With so much grace and happiness
Be proud just like the eagle.

Strut, strut just like the robin
Pleased with who you are
For no one can compare
To how memorable you are.

The Winds of Time

The winds of time have changed again,
I know not where they lead.
The universe requires a shift
from me and my serenity.

I labor to sail smoothly
through the gusts that play so cruelly.
But the force and strength of the winds of time
stretch my body into submission.

Where will you thrust me now this time?
Why do your arms wish to strain me?
Has not the passing of time been filled
with toiling urgencies?

I've bent and stretched just as you required.
I've even floated light in the sky
I've felt the pain of almost shattering
to reach your plateau Nirvana.

Goodbye My Love

Dedicated to my Aunt with love.

Day in day out I watch you sleep,
a sleep that keeps you far from me.
I try to reach you with my words,
but your sleep keeps you away from me.

Today I'll go to church and pray
that you will know I love you so.
God grant me this one gift I pray,
that I might share our love once more.

Journeying on my way to church,
I felt an urgency to see you first.
So I hurried to your bedside,
to let you know that I was here.

I held your hand and spoke to you,
"Severo, I love you,
now tell me that you love me too.
And with one last squeeze of my hand
he whispered with his dying breath,
"Maria, I love you too".

Chapter 3

The Hallow Moon

Tonight there's a full Hallow moon.
The night becomes eerie with gloom.
The clouds spread the sky
to show but a glimpse
of the moon easily hiding above.

The path through the woods becomes blocked.
The trees seem to gather and flock
like creatures in line
to be fed a main course.
I wonder if I'm the prime choice.

I feel the trees looking at me.
Their leaves gently flow just past me.
They cover my feet.
I feel a strange heat,
like something below touching me.

My mind tells me that I should run
from the strange clump of trees stopping me.
But my feet have grown roots
under the leaves,
gripping me fast to the ground.

My arms are now stretching up high,
entwining with darkness above.
I've developed a trunk
like the gathering trees
'neath the light of the glum Hallow moon.

The Road I See

I see that road in my dreams
sometimes the grass is green
other times it's white from the cold
but I see it just the same.
In the spring the trees are tall and green
in the winter they are bare and white,
from the chilling winds and brutal snow
that owns the seasons now.
I wished it would take me where
my dream tells me it goes.
To a cozy little farmhouse
I often dreamed I'd own.
A playful pinto running
wild in the pasture
feeling gay and euphoric
from the alphalfa it consumed.
A faithful dog sleeping
on the shady porch
lying by the lavenders,
swatting an unrelenting fly.
I think that this would be Heaven
just to be there a while
If I find that road I see in dreams
I'll make sure I'd never leave.

Maggie

A little ball of white fur,
you stole my heart away,
cuddly, rubbing close to me,
a source of energy
You always greet me with your love
whenever I come home,
and patiently wait for my return
with unconditional love.
You keep my feet warm when I read,
my shadow throughout the house.

You keep me company when I'm alone
and share my covers when I sleep.
When others have forsaken me,
you've always huddled near,
never barking without cause,
you know the rules I keep.
Better than a best friend,
I'd miss you even more,
for you've never questioned
my moods or ways,
you've loved me anyway.

Ode To The Donut

Mmm Mmm
I love the many donuts
I see in the glass case.
Especially the fat jelly ones
they mostly love me too.
For they will always call my name
so quietly, I alone can hear.
I always answer yes to them
and savor every bite.
Now when the jelly donuts
are nowhere to be found,
my next choice is the ever faithful
glazed donut with a hole.

But when I brought them
home with me, my grandson
said, "Oh look! My donut
has a hole in it, now what
am I going to do? Should I
go and look for it? How did
it just fall out?"
"Why don't we just go fill it up
with whip cream this first time?
Then jelly on the next one
and pudding on the last.
That's why there is a hole in it
to fill it with delight
and make it very special
for a very special child."

Hey Belle

Hey Belle, Hey Belle Hey Belle,
You're the orneriest dog I've ever seen
You keep on running away.
You just don't know how good it is
To have meals served through the day.

Hey Belle, Hey Belle, Hey Belle,
Your running away from who knows what
You sure a nasty dog
If you're not careful, you will wind up
On the bottom of a car's front tire.

Hey Belle, Hey Belle, Hey Belle
There you go again, Hey Belle,
Watch that car, Hey Belle
Your going to get tired, Hey Belle
Your going to go flat, Hey Belle
Hey Belle Hey Bell, Hey Belle,_--------------Hay Belle

I Like/Don't Like

I like candy
because it is sweet.
As sweet as you
It can't be beat.
I don't like peas,
they don't taste good,
just round and green
and hard to eat.
I like dogs
because their soft.
They love you back
and lick their paws.

I don't like snakes
because they're slimy,
and slither away
they look so *clammy*.
I like my bike.
It's red and shinny.
It goes real fast
on aired up tires.
But most of all,
I like my friend Charlie.
She makes me laugh
when I'm sad and cloudy.

DREAMSCAPE

Sitting on a puff of air
in the midst of endless twilight blue,
I fluffed the foggy mist
to cradle my head in dew.
I saw the sun strike its final splash of light
as it slowly surrendered peacefully behind the mountains,
and the moon in full magnitude
gracefully escaped to spread her light
across the land below.
Never had I felt such serenity, peace and tranquility.

I looked to one side of my puff of air
and saw a world in turmoil.
There were flashes of light, people screaming,
sounds of hatred and pain.
People crying, others killing,
why when we all are the same.
No children's laughter, just only sobbing.
No peace for them was here.
I cannot stand to see this misery. I have to look away.
I have such peace in this endless twilight.
I float past this instability.

I see others singing Christmas carols.
Their spirits free of pandemonium.
They pray for the ones at war.
Their hearts are with peace and love.
They almost reach my mist of air.
Their children filled with sounds of laughter
and kisses for their moms.
They can't comprehend the terror
on the other side of love.

And as I drift on, I see a room
filled with several men
and angry voices all talking at once,
but not in unison.
Declaring the war must go on,
yet, they never see the dying, or the mothers crying.
They never heard the children laughing
or the singing when it's done in harmony.
They are unable to seize the serenity
on the other side of hate.

So, I re-fluff my foggy mist, close my eyes
and cradle myself to sleep.

The Belle and the Cocker Spaniel

Belle Starr is a cuddly pup,
thinks she is the Queen.
She rules and reigns the family
she is the only pet.
She thinks she is allowed to do
anything she pleases.
She's a little dainty Bichon.
So careful where you walk or sit
she doesn't move an inch.
One day she had some company
her master's mother came to visit.
And with her was her Cocker Spaniel
she was extremely livid.

He went straight to Belle and tried to sniff her
"She growled and said, don't sniff me, yuck.
You're the one that smells so rank
Where have you been sleeping?"
"I sleep wherever I chose
I run the house at home
I've been running and
chasing opossums. A lot
more than you can do."

Oh posh! I can hunt
better than you, I just don't
like to smell like you.

Don't sit too close
you'll ruin my space.
I don't like you on my
pillow case."
You are a bitch
I heard them say
and by golly they were right."

"And you sir are no *blue blood*
and no one had to tell me that!"

As We Grow

I once knew a girl on a swing,
she would like to have everything.
So she wished on a star,
then she wished on a cloud,
but she still did not have anything.
HA! HA!
There once was a boy on a pony,
thought he was the fastest around.
So he whipped his grand pony,
To make it run faster,
but found himself flat on the ground.
HO! HO!

So if you are lazy and don't won't to think,
and expect all your needs will come when you click.
Don't lift a finger and see what you get,
it might be pain, hunger and sorrow.

And if you're a boy on a shiny black horse,
who whips him till he falls from exhaustion.
Be wary small boy, because as you grow
your tumbles hurt more than exhaustion.

When I Was Young

When I was young, I knew
a place
where the waters ran clean
and free.
The only pain was scraping
your knee
and a band-aid was the remedy.

When I was young all trees
were tall
and reached the blue, blue sky,
and the only pain when
climbing a tree
was when Mom or Dad
found out.

When I was young, I'd
journey far
where the grass was green
and mowed.
The only pain was hearing
Mom scold
when my knees were soiled
and green.

When I was young, wherever
I'd go
Mom and Dad were near,
and thanks to them, I grew
up strong
and safe from life's debris.

Stinky but Okay

Stinky but okay?
Don't know who could pass that criteria today,
except perhaps a little handsome fella,
that had the females swooning some years ago.

He was rather dark haired and shiny
with a streak of white hair floating
wild and shaggy across his face.

He loved the dark-haired felines that met his likeness
with a white streak down their back.
He had to chase the ladies
for he had to reach them quickly to tantalize them
before his odor did.

To him it was appealing
to them less than intriguing
until he captured them
and began his courting game.
His words would hypnotize them
like "Ah my beautiful flower
let me show you how purrrr . . . fect you are."

So he romanced them playfully and flattered them intensely
and stroked their fur till they purred nonstop.
They soon forgot about the odor
and were left grinning cheek to cheek
and they all were left watching him
as he turned his back to leave.
"It's the way they look when they leave"
his lady would reply; and he'd
waggle his tail as he strutted to his next challenging affair
for little high flying Pepe Le Pew,
which by the way was his name,
always left his ladies purring and meowing
"Come back Pepe Le Pew! Come back!"

Raging River/Placid Waters

Flowing river
placid waters
harbor many
untold creatures,
plants, arbors
and waters
of all color

And sizes
change daily
with the seasons
to mask
a new reason
for each picture
that we see.

River raging
resting place
to cradle many
known and unknown
whichever you
chose to be
sleeping place

Hidden forever
the River has
many faces
tranquil to rage
each has its place
beauty abounds
its shores
To choose
the view that satisfies you
like hues
that ripen
as the seasons
change.

Resolution

The word resolution
is misinterpreted
with diminished power from flippant use.

Let's remember
wishful thinking and indecision
does not make the grade.

A resolution is a declaration,
a tenacious and relentless goal
filled with fortitude and dedication.

It's a word misconstrued.

Red

I would like to fly high on a red kite
and visit whoever lives up in the clouds
would we have tea and cookies
or misty fizz and air filled tarts?
I want to find out which ones.
I'd like to have a red boat
that could go deep in the Red Sea.
We'd dive so deep we'd be the first
to see the different forms of life
in a city under the sea.
Red is such an impressive color.
It excites and announces itself profoundly,
creating prolific ideas and zealous attire;
red can invent and control whatever you see.
That is why I chose a red kite
to fly to the top of the floating clouds
where else could we have misty fizz
and air filled tarts as tea and cookies.
Only a red boat could dive so deep
to capture the sights beyond the sea,
visit a city forever lost
beyond the natural realm.
Red lights up the world
and strengthens all within it.
Flaunting its color filled with power.
There is no other to compare.

Little Texican

I am just a little ⁱTexican
paying the most of the taxes I can,
so I can drive to Nuevo Leon
going as fast as the ⁱⁱ*nieve* can fall.
Aye, what am I thinking about?
No snow in this ⁱⁱⁱTejano land,
just wind and heat.
^{iv}*Aye que calor*!
That's what we have
on the Tejano plain.
I wanted to go to America
but America don't want me.
Just wanted to work for some ^v*dinero*
to buy a ^{vi}*ranchito chiquito.*

I wanted to have little goats and ^{vii}*shicans*
to lay some eggs for ^{viii}*desayuno.*
But America, she still say no.
So *Mejico* here I go.

Here I go back to *Mejico*
to try to buy land for me,
but now they have this giant wall,
ju know like in East Alemania.

The one it took years to tear down.
Now we have one standing on Mexican ground.
Why do we have a wall like that?
We are neighbors, we should be like [ix]*hermanos.*

We're just little *Texicans*
We don't want to fight.
We have been neighbors for many years,
we don't terrorize your land.
the land we want to live on.
You let the Chinese, Japanese, Pakistanis,
Vietnamese, Arabs and others all buy
land in jur America.
But the little *Texican* no.
We don't make bombs,
we just work hard to pay
jur taxes.
Goodbye America,
the land of the free
the little *Texican* cries

who now loves *jur* soil
but has to say Goodbye
to the *Tejano* land
and find a way to stay in *Mexico* . . .

Or maybe not.

What Have You Done To America?

What's happening to America
The land of the free?
Is it all a hoax when we say
"We the people of the United States"
while the congressmen threaten each other
and hold "we the people" hostage to their will.
It feels like terrorism to be able to
hold the President at bay,
blocking his healthcare reform law
from the poor, disabled, seniors
and unemployed waiting for relief.

Barak Obama was voted President,
but why the name calling
where's the support?
Is this the birth of a new America
now losing the Brave?
All I see is shallow insensitive beings
who don't care for their country or fellowman.

What happened to Justice and Liberty for All.
It shames me to see the President put down
A man who was voted and placed in office to lead.
Where is his power, was it ever his?
Who runs this country?
The lobbyists and the chosen few.
Are we one country
Or are we two, Reds and Blue
Who do you chose?

Through their hunger for power
men in suits have brought
shame and disgrace for what we were.
The wise men have fallen and lost their sight
Their minds have closed and refused the light.
"We the people" said we trusted this man
The one that speaks for us and leads with an iron hand.

So let the President lead and carry our torch
This is America, I believe we are still free.
Quit acting like bullies.
Or saloon hussies and . . .
Dust yourselves off.

Just follow the leader
It will be alright
But look what you've done to America?
My Country . . . I Love.

The Promised Gift

Did you know the road to Heaven was all jagged and tom?
Did you know the road to Heaven had pot holes and slopes?
Did you know there would be no street lamps to guide you
or a sign by the road to show you which way to go.
Did you know? Did you know?

Did you know there would be little traffic to hurry you on
your way,
Or a friendly traveler to help you, if you should stray?
Did you know the road was full of danger, when you offered
help to strangers?
Did you know? Did you know?

Did you know the snakes, thorns, and rocks that hurt you as you
travel on, just brought you another mile closer to the Glory to be
revealed.
Did you think receiving the Lord Jesus as your savior
would protect you from all trouble?
Did you think that all it meant was you would be free of struggle,
that life would be much simpler, and almost without toil?

Just remember, every drop of blood and sweat we excrete in
His Name,
brings us closer to the final mile to receive His promised Gift,

Why I'll Never Know

Since I was just a little girl,
I learned how strange the world could be.
I loved the magical gifts it'd bring
surprising me with its jubilant treats.

The colors were the most enticing
wonders that would draw me nearer.
Some were cool, smooth and damp
while others were hot and exciting.

I learned that too much love would hurt
unknowingly a small young delicate pet
when held too tight and often;
and that no love could also damage
but why, I never knew.

I saw how people shunned each other
for reasons I shall never know.
Maybe they won't ever care
why they spurned the other.

A fluffy, frilly brand knew dress
would fill young girls to greedy tantrums.
Yet a critically ill frail human being
would stir them to ridicule
What makes the human race so fascinating,
yet painfully unpredictable?
Will they react in kindness
or play on rage and mockery?

What makes a couple pledge their love
bear children, yet still trade their love for another?
While an animal in the wild keeps his loyalty?
How does it all make sense; this carousel of colors?

Maybe the world rotates too fast,
or maybe when we're on our heads
we get a blood rush to our brain,
I know I have no answers.

Is it possible we're just a lower species,
but think we are superior beings,
simply because we can form an occasional lucid thought,
yet still preside in the company of ignorance.

Rosa

She sat alone on the school steps while the sun lazily showed its face. The breeze was cool and rather biting, so she wrapped her arms tight around her knees. Rosa had to start school in a new neighborhood and learn a new language. Meantime, the sun took its time to warm the earth. It did not show bright at all.

Rosa was only 5 years old, not able to speak English, surrounded by a world that was different. She had many reasons to be afraid.

Slowly the children began to arrive, but all they did was stare. Rosa could not speak to them or understand their words. She did know they were laughing at her, so she just looked away.

A teacher finally came to her and asked her name. Little Rosa just shook her head, and the kids all laughed. The teacher than asked, "*Su nombre?*" She then replied, "*Me llamo Rosa.*" Again the kids began to laugh.

When it was finally time for lunch, the sun was shining bright and warm. She found a quiet spot to sit and eat. A little freckled, red-haired girl came and sat by her side.

"Hi, I'm Sheila," she said. "They like to laugh at me too. I guess my red hair and freckles make me different like you."

Rosa looked confused at first; then Sheila pointed to her hair. Rosa grinned just a little, and then Sheila pointed to her cheeks. Rosa smiled a great big smile exposing her missing teeth. Rosa then began to grin till it turned into a laugh, for Sheila's two front teeth were also missing; both girls couldn't help but laugh out loud with their similar toothless grins.

It's not too hard to find similarities in everyone we meet. We just have to be willing to look a little bit.

The Adventures of Rosita

Rosa never quite fit in that Lutheran elementary school. She finished the first grade but did not want to continue. She always felt left out and never included in the fun games they played outside. She just never knew what to say to make the girls laugh. The girls that could make the other kids laugh were the popular ones. Nobody ever knew if she was around much less listen to what she had to say. When school was out she would walk to her grandmother's house. She liked to visit her grandmother and grandfather. Papa Chano was tall, happy and liked to sing. He was always doing something for us to enjoy after school. Mama Chole would prepare the piano lessons for the girls, except me. I asked, "Mama Chole, why won't you teach me to play the piano?" She would throw up her hands and chuckle, oh Rosita, you are too young. Wait until you grow another year or two."

Rosita screamed "Two"! She tried to hold back the tears but could not. The older girls giggled and would glance a look or two at her. Rosita may have been a young child, but she was more assertive and alert than the other children. She sat quietly behind her grandmother so that she could not see her and listened to what lessons she was teaching the big girls. They were not interested and had short attention spans. They did not like the lessons that took them too long to learn. After a while Mama Chole would say "Bueno, tengo hambre. Let's go to the store to buy a few things I need to prepare the caldo. Papa Chano and Mama Chole always made caldos. I think because it would feed more people than a regular meal and everybody would wind up at dinner time. I always stayed hungry because I did not like most of the vegetables and for them the more vegetables the better. Most of the soups were all vegetables. My favorite was the chicken soup with potatoes, and corn on the cob. Yum! Then we would add salsa and corn tortillas. While grandmother and the girls went to the store, Rosita sat on the piano and began to practice. She was so surprised she could play the first two songs in the book and sing-a-long. She was sitting and singing when Mama Chole and the girls returned. Papa Chano had been standing in a dark corner listening to her practice.

"Well, what is this?" Mama Chole exclaimed.

"The runt stole the others thunder," said Papa Chano. "Atta girl, I think you were teaching the wrong one".

Mama Chole said, "Aye mija. Do that again so I can see if you have done it right."

Rosa sat up tall and proud and played her two little songs she just learned with a great big smile.

Mama Chole put her hands on her hips and shook her head. "I'm so impressed. I better set a time to teach you first."

Rosita felt like she was finally noticed but she was always in her grandfather's eye. Playing music was the one thing Rosita wanted to know the best. Music brought so much emotion when she heard it and played it. She didn't need any friends when she was playing music.

The Honking and the Fury

In the summertime, my sister and I were dropped off at my grandparent's house to be babysat until they got off work. This was difficult at times for me because we were second generation Mexican-Americans. I understood Spanish but did not like to speak it because the older kids made fun of my accent. My Grandmother spoke only Spanish but understood English and my Grandfather was prolific in both languages. It was always exciting to visit them because you never knew what new adventure you would have because Grandpa was always involved in different kinds of projects. I used to like that, but since my Grandfather had bought this huge goose that was meaner than a guard dog, we all had to keep our toes ready to run. Our shoes stayed on and we would whisper when we were outside, hoping he did not find us. After eating breakfast, we were all told to go outside and play and to stay outside for the whole day. My grandmother and my aunts were having a bible study and said we would mess the house up, so we were to stay outside and if we wanted water, to drink from the faucet.

Today that might have been grounds for child neglect and the spankings we got would have been close to child abuse, but back then we never heard those words or even knew they would be grounds to get even if you wanted too. My Dad was a Principal, teacher, and coach at a country school near a border town in Texas and my mother worked for the Court House typing up court cases. I was proud of both of them and their jobs. For being bilingual and educated it was still difficult to earn a good living. An instead of being sought for your talents you were looked down for your skin color. Well, I may as well get on with it. Since I was the youngest, I was thrown out on the front porch first and my sister and two cousins would then hurriedly lock the front door. I would stand by the door trying to pull it open again. I whispered at the top of my voice begging, please let me come in. It's going to eat me. My cousins Miguel and Ricky were laughing and yelling, "Hurry and run up the tree before it knows you are there."

"No!" I whispered back at the top of my lungs. "Let me in!"

Just then Sara came running to the door. "Hurry Rosa, Mama Chloe is coming and she is angry. So hurry so we can run after you climb the tree."

I hurried as quietly to the end of the porch and tried to see if the goose was under the porch, but I did not see it. So I took a deep breath and began running to the mulberry tree as fast as I could. Just before I reached the tree I heard the goose honking. I took a flying leap for the higher branch of the tree and swung my legs up and held on tight. The goose was running in circles honking and flapping its wings, trying to pinch my legs with its beak. My grandfather had clipped its wings so it could not fly away, but it could take high jumps or what we called short flights. Grandpa just figured we would get a running edge on the mean old goose, but when he wanted to he could jump up and pinch our toes and legs. I finally got my balance on the tree and climbed up higher. Ricky came out next swinging a broom at the goose and holding Sara's hand. He grabbed her by the waist and lifted her up to a tall branch and then he jumped up and climbed the tree like a monkey at the zoo. Only Miguel was left in the house. He began to cry to abuelita. "They won't let me play with them." All of us on the tree sat there with our mouth wide open in disbelief. "Grandma, he's lying." The three of us yelled.

She said, "No, I believe you three are lying. Look at this poor boy crying because you hurt his feelings by not letting him play. Wait until your grandfather gets here and I tell him what you have done." She turned to Miguel, "come on with me mijo" You can play inside since they are being mean to you. Okay"

"Okay", he said with a pouty face, then turned and made an ugly face to me and my sister and cousin.

When Grandpa came home, Miguel put his pouty face back on and managed to cry a tear at Grandpa. Grandpa reached in his pocket and pulled out a lollipop and said there, there Mijo. Then he turned and winked at us still sitting in the tree. The goose was still honking and flapping its wings at us. Then the goose noticed an old man coming down the alley. When he reached our gate and came in, the goose turned and began to chase the old man with a cane. The old man turned and ran out the gate with the goose chasing him down the alleyway. Halfway down the alley the man threw the cane at the goose and the goose flapped its wings and jumped on the old man knocking him down. The goose then seemed satisfied and left the man to chase other innocent passersby. We stayed sitting in the tree laughing so hard at the honking goose. Grandpa new that goose would chase that man, but he just sat there and waited to see what would happen. I think that grandpa did not like the man.

While the goose was gone we all climbed out of the tree and ran to the porch where Papa Chano made us some Raspas; Frosties to the rest of the non-Spanish speaking world.

Chapter 4

Kites

It was a cool brisk spring day when we put our box kites together after arguing about who would get to chose their colors first. It was becoming a family tradition to explore the many kite designs and which ones would fly the best. This year it would be the box kite. The box kite was always the hardest for me to get in the air, but once flying, it could fly so high and grand.

The wind would push it down to the ground at first, as if to wound it purposefully, so that it could not succeed. Sometimes the more effort given

to escape the tricks of the wind would only bring it crashing down harder to the ground and splinter its sticks so that it could not continue. However, some would escape the sudden whips of the wind. If you kept still and waited for just the right breeze you could let your string go and the kite would be able to lift suddenly, to the next altitude, as if mastering a game and moving to the next level. As the wind would catch it, again it would struggle, trying not to be forced down again.

Sometimes it would be better to shorten its string, but when the time was right, you could let it reach its greatest height to succeed.

Rolling Green Hills

There was an appealing little town
named Rolling Green Hills.
It had beauty and charm,
this quaint town that drew
many new residents to stay.
But as it is, all good things come to an end,
and the winds of time begin to change.
A new family from outside the states moved in
which might have caused havoc and terror
to a somewhat peaceful little town.
The first night a neighbor's dog was found mutilated.
The next night a child turned up missing from her crib.
The town's people were in shock
and held a town meeting to say.
"Woe be it to us if we don't find
who is causing this horror?"

The town's people asked,
"Please give any information to who this person might be."
Then suddenly the wind began to shift
and the doors to the meeting hall blew open.
The sound the wind spoke was,
"The Omeada family," then the doors closed again.
The Omeada family turned to run
but the crowd was on them in seconds.
Without a sound before the next word was said,
the Omeada family lay dead,
father, mother, daughter and son.

The next morning the men took
the Omeada family to the cemetery,
the one beyond the Rolling Green Hills,
to the Rolling Brown Hill Cemetary.
The people of Rolling Green Hills felt safe
with the Omeada's gone,
but then the third night brought reality back.
A newly wed was found murdered and put to flames.
The people wondered now what would they do?
With the fourth night coming, the thought of
what would come next made them tremble.
So they all took a weapon and met in the meeting hall again.
They all looked at each other with grave suspicion
prepared to take a life. Again they asked for help
in finding who this murder could be, and again,
The wind began to shift and made the sound
look at your neighbor to your right.
Then the doors slammed again and the
friendly people of Rolling Green Hills
slowly turned to their right and with fear in their eyes
began to shoot, stab, bludgeon their neighbor
until all were dead or dying.

No longer was the peaceful placid town known as
Rolling Green Hills but instead The Rolling Red Hills
of Death by Massacre.

It's The Women's Job To Prod

Well, it's another morning and the lights in the kitchen still don't work. Maybe today is the day a revelation will happen and he'll remember to fix them.

The day continues, time keeps passing. So I say. "Honey, could you fix the kitchen lights today?"

He says, "Oh yea, I got all I need to get it done."

I've heard that once too many times, so I know I'll have to prod him, at least one more time.

Maybe if I feed him lunch, he'll remember to get it done. So I say, "How's about a tuna fish sandwich before you get started?"

"Hey, that sounds good to me."

So I fix him the sandwich while he watches TV. I put some chips along for the ride and pour him a drink of soda to boot. He seems content with it all. Then he says, "Can I have seconds this sandwich is so good." So I hustle and get him seconds too. But when he is through, he continues to sit and watch the television.

Oh no, I recognize that sound. He's starting to snore. So I say, "Honey, should I wait to do the dishes or can you get started to fix the lights?"

"Huh? Oh go ahead and wash the dishes, I'll start those lights after you're through."

Boy, I left myself wide open for that one I know, but I'm gonna get him on the next round for sure.

I finished the dishes as quick as I could, but I hear the snoring coming from the chair by the TV again.

So I yell. "Okay, I'm finished! Your turn! And he says, "Huy? What? Oh Okay." He gets up slowly and stretches his back. Then like a prisoner that gets a reprieve from the governor,the phone rings and it's his mother. Another hour I wait. I got to hold fast before another month passes. My lights will work today and with no blood spilling.

He hangs up the phone and starts heading for the chair as he tells me what his mother had to say. I say, "Here! You were working on the lights dear, don't you remember?"

"The lights," he says, "oh yes, let's see. I'll have them done in no time, you'll see."

So, I left him alone and did my chores. I'd see him every now and then going in and out of the house. When night time fell, I was tired and had forgotten about the kitchen lights and if they were working or not. It would be too late to hassle him now. So I chose not to ask if it was done. He then comes to me. "Did you notice the lights?"

"Oh,the lights? No. Did you get it done?" I reluctantly asked.

So he flicked the switch and the kitchen shined so bright. He had fixed the lights that I had done without for maybe over 6 months. All I had to do was hassle him, till he got it done. And he did it so well. I told him well-done.

Now what was the next project? Oh yea . . .

Feliz Navidad

The season is ripe, ready and festive.
The children are running on sugar mode
and Santa Claus adrenaline.
Mothers try to keep up
but are running on caffeine
sharing their children's high
Excited and baking
the cookies at night
but sneaking some extra bites.
All mothers are doing
their ethnic traditions,
like eggnog, press cookies
and apple pie.
Another is making tamales con salsa
y pasteles de fruta. Oh boy.
Others are bringing the ale out
and dancing to the festive music.
Some are singing praises to God,
but we are all rejoicing.
In one way or another
we are all celebrating
the day the Savior was born.
So let's not forget to say
HAPPY BIRTHDAY TO YOU
JESUS! HOORAY!

Lost Love

on the edge of the cliff
the waves crash on the rocks
our time quickly passing
like the sand in an hour glass.
our love shortly lived
yet exuberantly savored
we would start everyday
on the edge of the cliff.

(Palindrome : Poem that can be read frontwards and
backwards with meaning)

Game Over

The demons of Hell have definitely found me, she thought as she slowly opened her eyes, looking at a cheap motel room. She reeked of alcohol and stale perfume. How could her demons *not* find her? She was alone in a disheveled bed. Apparently, there had been a restless night.

No one else appeared to be in the room. At least this room was better than what she had found herself flying in a few days ago. She was becoming accustomed to waking up in a gutter of filth; soiled, torn clothing and needle tracks in her arms, infected with blistered sores.

The Devil lay by her side many times and grinned at his prize. All it took was to offer a dream that had too high a price to pay. Low self-esteem and injected courage to catch his victim was all it took to make a win. How easy a game is the prize of a soul?

She was still under the influence of what she partook in that night. She wondered, *How did I get here?* She had no purse, money or identification. She began to cry. "Where am I?"

She saw her face in the mirror. It was like looking at herself for the first time. She saw a woman in her 30's with ratted, dried-looking gray hair. Her skin appeared leathered and hardened. Her eyes smoldered deep in her face, with no light or color evident. Her lips were also gray and dull.

She continued to stare at the woman in the mirror, as if she did not know who she was. She lifted her hands to touch her face, like there was a mistake, but her hands felt the rough skin.

She then pulled out debris from her hair. She thought, *My God who am I? How long have I been this way? It has to be a dream. I couldn't be that woman.*

She turned away from the mirror. That's when she saw a woman lying facedown on the bed. Her clothing torn, her right arm outstretched, showing needle tracks and scars. Her face looked aged beyond her years. She lay motionless, reflecting the abuse she and others had rendered to her now lifeless body.

She cried, "What's happening? Who is she? How did I get here?"

She flashed back to the earliest memory she could recall. She remembered going to her first junior high dance, where she met her first boyfriend and fell in love. There and then she was introduced to her first joint, which she reluctantly took. She then eagerly progressed to whites, Quaaludes, and then sped on to meth; but her drug of choice—and sure delight—was lovely heroin. She had stolen and lied to the ones that cared for her with no remorse and continued traveling on her course. She now remembered swapping body treasures for drunken pleasures; trusting in friends who paid her off with tainted drugs and used her body till there was no breath left. No, this could not be happening.

She then turned to the mirror again, as if the reflection would change. Through her tears she saw a small child with long, black hair and an innocent face. Her eyes still had the look of hope and want looking back at her.

"Don't you remember me, Sally? I went with you on that first dance. I'm the one that told you no, but you must not have heard me at all. That smoke made my head feel funny and made me

have to lie to Mommy and Daddy. It made me feel like I was worthless, lying and sneaking behind their backs.

"Then you thought whites were the best. They'd give you more energy to stay up late. You'd have to drink some liquor to bring you down. You liked it all and never thought; Sally, this is more than just a game. You are now a full-time user. You didn't finish school or hold down a job. You cared about no one, just getting the next drug. You lied, cheated, and stole for whatever you needed. Isn't this what you chose for us?"

"Who are you?" Sally screamed.

The girl in the mirror began to laugh. "Why, I'm you, Sally. Don't you recognize me?"

"No. You can't be me. I'm . . ."

"You're what?" the girl in the mirror interrupted. "Smarter, wiser, prettier ? *What?*" she yelled.

The little girl began to fade into darkness, and the woman's face reappeared in the mirror.

"Look at us now, Sally," the voice from the mirror echoed. "You've wasted our time, like a child engulfed in a video game, and now there are no `do-overs` left. We've lost our chance to succeed with pride and to cleanse our soul. I'm you when you were new, and she's you when it is all said and done. All that is left is the fluorescent light flashing our fate: *Game Over.*"

Trembling, Sally felt a presence behind her. She slowly turned to face her eyes on a hideous creature. She had seen that face before. She thought perhaps in a dream, but now she knew he owned her soul. She lowered her head and went with the creature she had served all her short life. She knew she had shamed herself and her loved ones and, mostly, had betrayed God. She now had to pay the price. She was bound to continue doing her hideous acts, for she was branded for eternity to serve the Beast—with no way out.

The Photograph

Looking at this photograph
Hanging on the wall,
A memory that was brought back
From a time I prefer not to recall.

There are four of us posing
Leaning on an old fallen tree
We never glanced at each other
We held tight to our attitude
As the fallen dead dry stained bark did.
We also held dead our emotions.

Still on this beautiful sunny mild chilled day
We were told to lineup and smile for the photograph.
We were all related through marriage but
That was the only bond.

We were all so different we didn't care
To even wonder what was on the others mind,
But we all knew, the girl on the right was crazy
She liked to fight, no reason needed
That made her so content
Even more than drinking worm Tequila.

The next girl never had much too say
She never went near the others.
It was best to pretend that
You were alone and to Hell
with all the others.
She'd act like so what
She knew she couldn't believe
Whatever was being said.

The next one was the trouble maker
She would stir the wind of toil and trouble with no effort at all.
The last seemed like she never could
Figure out what was going on.
When Girl#1 would yell in her face
It was because she had been herded through lies.
By Girl #3 who just was bored and wanted to get it started.

And when Girl#1 would get into
Girl#2 face, their sometimes would be
A ruckus. It wasn't always
Pretty but there were times
They would combine there
Thoughts and scare the others.

Not to often though just when
They had dogs and horses in common.
Those were strange days and unusual
Circumstances.

And though 35 years have already passed
Some divorced, others are gone
We still remain emotionally sterile
But our children still try to reach us
And find the history of the
Girls leaning on the fallen tree.

Her Heart

Her heart was ripe and full for the taking.
She offered it free with no strings or cages.
He thought he was hidden behind a façade
concealing the truthfulness of his desires.

He laughed to himself when he thought he had taken
her heart that was pure, but it still was not shaken
by his smile or his touch nor his debonair way,
for she was aware of his two-sided ways.

Though she was fresh and new to exploring,
her mind was still wise and vigil not failing.
She slowly stepped in and tested the waters,
saying, "I find you quite cold and deceiving."

He answered, "Wait, wait, how can you decide
when you've not given me a little more time
to reach you or show you how pleasing I'll be,
if you let me touch you, I'll please you, you'll see."

"No, no!" she replied. "That's not what I mean.
I can see you don't carry the strengths that I need,
to be honest, faithful, righteous and whole.
Be gone! Don't expect me to excuse what you are."

Her heart had been free and ready to conquer.
His character fell short, not good for the taking.
No charges or pledges, no catches or ties
yet he failed to convince her
she saw his disguise.

The Journal

One day while walking in the park, I came across a journal. Someone had left it lying on a bench facing the fountain. I noticed right away the book had no owner's name, ID, or markings. So I turned the page and began to read what was written in bold black ink, precise and clear.

Stunned at first by what I read, it grasped my heart and throat. I began to feel tears well up inside my eyes.

I read again:

Today is the day I've been waiting for.
Today is the day I shall die.
I've waited too long in this hurtful world;
I believe it's time I went home.

For once I feel such energy,
I'm sure I'm doing right.
No more catty looks or malicious undertones
will I have to pretend I didn't see or hear.

I'll dress in my best formal gown,
the one I never wore.
Fix up my hair and paint my face
with my best tones and shades.

It'll be like prom night.
But no one will notice I'm bland.
No one needs to speak to me
to notice I've nothing to add.

I'll put on my best perfume.
I'll have the fragrance of a flower.
My best shoes will have to do;
I only have one pair to wear.
I think a glass of wine
is definitely in order for tonight.
For this will be my final night
to face the pain of living.

I'll toast the moon and say goodbye
to all who ever listened.
It'll be so grand, quite a soirée,
you'll wish you hadn't missed it.

Well, I better get busy now;
I wouldn't want to be late.
Who knows who I'll meet
while I travel on to a kinder
more appealing world?

I have no choice, I'll wave goodbye,
as I float out of my body.
No one will care or miss me here,
there'll be no tears shed for me.

I'm free at last to be a part
of what life has kept from me.

As I finished reading this tormented story, my eyes kept filling up with tears. My heart felt the pressure of a stone. Who was this girl in misery? Could I have made a difference? Would I have tried to help her, or just looked away?

I grasped the book close to my chest and hid it in my coat. And as I began to walk away, a timid young girl did show. As she slowly walked to the bench, I discreetly spoke to her. "Did you lose something?"

Her eyes looked at the bench and all around it, "I thought I had, but I think not. No!" she shook her head and said, "I just came here to sit and watch the beautiful fountain flow."

Her eyes then rose to meet mine and I sensed a kinship then; feeling a connection with this lost and wandering soul. I felt an urgency to reach her, so I asked her if we could speak.

"You see, I come here every week. It's where my daughter and I would meet. She would save her Sundays to be our Special Day. We'd go see a movie or go to dinner, but often we'd just shop. She was killed in an accident one day, as I waited for her here. I still come on Sundays, just to visit with her. Do you mind joining us this very Special Day?"

The girl replied, "Oh no, I would love your company. That would be so nice. For today has turned into a Special Day, for me just visiting with you. I felt it in my soul that something would happen today and I was right; it truly is a very Special Day."

"You know, I had that feeling too. We must both be kindred hearts. Let's go get a bite to eat and see a movie too."

"I think we shall be good friends," the younger did reply. "We'll meet here on Sundays and visit for a while. Then we'll see a movie and grab some munchies too. We'll have such fun, I know we will. I'll hate the day to end, but now I know I'll see you anytime you need to call, and you, in turn, will see me before I take a fall."

Lonely From Now On

Lonely I've become these sleepless nights.
There is no connection or pleasure to the light,
yet I still see your beguiling smile as you shine
like you always did, making me sparkle with the wine.
How did we get from there to here?
When I choose, I see your face everywhere.
Closing my eyes, I can then feel your breath
from our bewitching, enslaving kiss and caress.
Laughter and teasing is all I remember
as we started each day that December.
How loved I felt back then
when we played life as a game.

Now I wait for you to visit me
in my dreams, but I can't sleep.
What a sad predicament of the night
and the sun that keeps you from the light.
Were we too much in love, we used up our time?
We always strutted around like we were fine.
You made me feel completely bold
I hope I made you feel as whole.

When The Clock Chimes Gong

The clock is racing faster
I hear its nonmelodic tic
and a second later the closing tock.
My time is running out.
I cannot rush with the others
and do a good job. It appears
rugged and without time.
I tell myself it is alright,
don't worry. You'll
make the grade alright.
Just close your eyes and
dream how when you close
Your eyes you'll see,
You're loving mother waiting for you.
Don't fear what you don't see
or cry for what you don't know
it's just the world clock ticking
to prepare you for your trip.
I'm so tired, I can't even see.
Help me put some sense in this
I don't care what you try to be.
Just be it well and with feeling.
I'll see you when the clock chimes Gong
I'm the one running to face my Maker.

Route 66

Girls like her don't know when to stop,
they go on and on about all they got.
They borrow your man for a one-night shot;
then smile at you proudly, like they go a lot.

But girls like me can't begin where they end,
we can't fall in love and then just pretend,
that what she has borrowed was just a night's fling,
while her smile echoes loudly in my mind and I scream.

Girls like her get carried away,
by all the attention, she's drawn in that way.
She grows stronger and stronger with each man she takes,
and smiles to the ones left behind in a rage.

But girls like her will someday be crushed,
by someone like me, who's just had enough,
and that's when I'll cheer and finally forget,
the smile that was left as she's carried away.

So Baby, Baby if you think that she's hot,
go ahead and see what she's got,
but remember that I won't be waiting in line,
while you get your kicks traveling on Route 66.

The Clock
By Melba Peña

The time is drawing near
When the seconds of the clock
Won't be sounding for you.

The time is coming soon
When the closing of my door
Won't be opening for you.

Cuz the nighttime comes too quickly
And the sunlight fails to shine,
And my words just seem to echo
Through the shadows of your heart.

I can't believe you go,
Without a second thought
To the sounding of your roar.

I can't believe you leave
Without looking back to see
The pain you're leaving me

Cuz the rain that comes so quickly
Will one day with thunder roar,
And the lightening flash will blind me
from the love that once was yours.

We'll slowly turn away in silence
As the winds begin to wail,
And the time will finally come
When the seconds of the clock
Will sound no more for you.

Run

You're so mean
You face is green
You look like a fellow in an alien scene.

You kicked so high
You missed my eye
You fell to the ground with a howling cry.

Yea, yea, yea, yea yea
You make me laugh
Yea, yea, yea, yea, yea
You're so mean.

You raise your hand
,to strike at me
But you hit the door with a burning heat.

You screeched in pain.
You yelled my name.
But there's a bolt on the door with a heavy chain.

Your days are done.
Your games no fun.
Runaway, the cops now are on their way.

They'll play your game.
You'll feel the pain
So you'd better get to running boy

It's now your turn to
run, run, run, run, run
I hear the sirens now.

run, run run run. run
I see the flashing lights
Run . . .

You're history boy.
Run . . .
They'll treat you right.
Run . . . .
Good-bye
Run . . . .
Good riddance.

Winter

A wonderful season
with magnificent splendor
and preparation for rebirth.
Illusion of dying
by freezing winds
with finalization
by the freezing rain.
Colors of the sky
resemble the ground.
Sometimes the sun
rises like the sound of a cymbal
duplicating its bright color
to the snow on the ground.
Before long the frozen branches
of a tree will break off
to emphasize the possibility
of final demise.

No longer is there any vibrant color on the bark,
and the sun again hides its face to the dark.
Thus the world continues
through this cycle of time
till the sun one day
turns its face to glow
its golden hue to the land below.
The ice begins to melt,
some with crackling remorse,
that its season of life will now emerge
until the sun turns its face again.
But for now the broken leafless tree
will stretch out to greet the sun,
and the illusion of death will dissipate for now.